Little One,
We Knew You'd Come

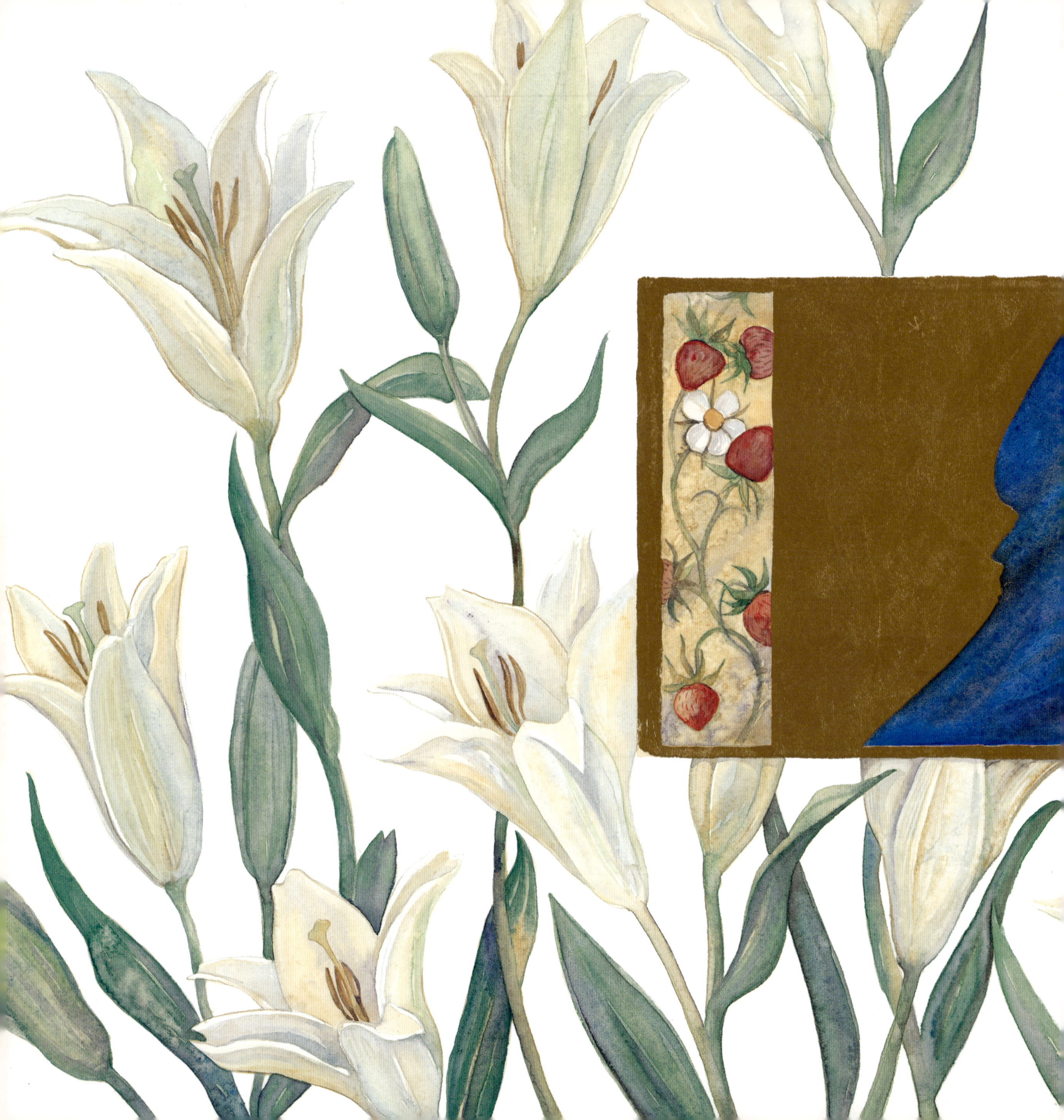

Little One, We Knew You'd Come

Sally Lloyd-Jones

Illustrated by **Jackie Morris**

*for Pam
with best wishes
Jackie Morris*

FRANCES LINCOLN
CHILDREN'S BOOKS

Text copyright © Sally Lloyd-Jones 2006
Illustrations copyright © Jackie Morris 2006

This edition published in the UK in 2006 by
Frances Lincoln Children's Books, 4 Torriano Mews,
Torriano Avenue, London NW5 2RZ
www.franceslincoln.com

First published in the USA in 2006 by Little, Brown and Company

All rights reserved

No part of this publication may be reproduced, stored in a retrieval system,
or transmitted, in any form, or by any means, electrical, mechanical,
photocopying, recording or otherwise without the prior
written permission of the publisher or a licence permitting
restricted copying. In the United Kingdom such licences
are issued by the Copyright Licensing Agency,
Saffron House, 6-10 Kirby Street, London EC1N 8TS.

British Library Cataloguing in Publication Data
available on request

ISBN 10: 1-84507-731-8
ISBN 13: 978-1-84507-731-0

Illustrated with watercolour and gold leaf

Set in Papyrus

Printed in China

1 3 5 7 9 8 6 4 2

For Harry, Eleanor, Olivia,
Jonathan, and Emily –
I'm so glad you came!
— S.L.J.

To Kath and Ella
And to mothers everywhere
— J.M.

Little one,
    we knew you'd come.

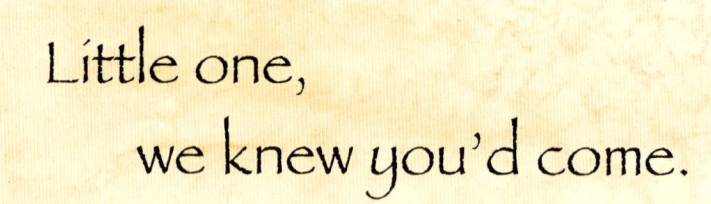

We hoped. We dreamed. We watched for you.
We counted the days till you were due.
We waited. How we longed for you,

And the day that you were born.

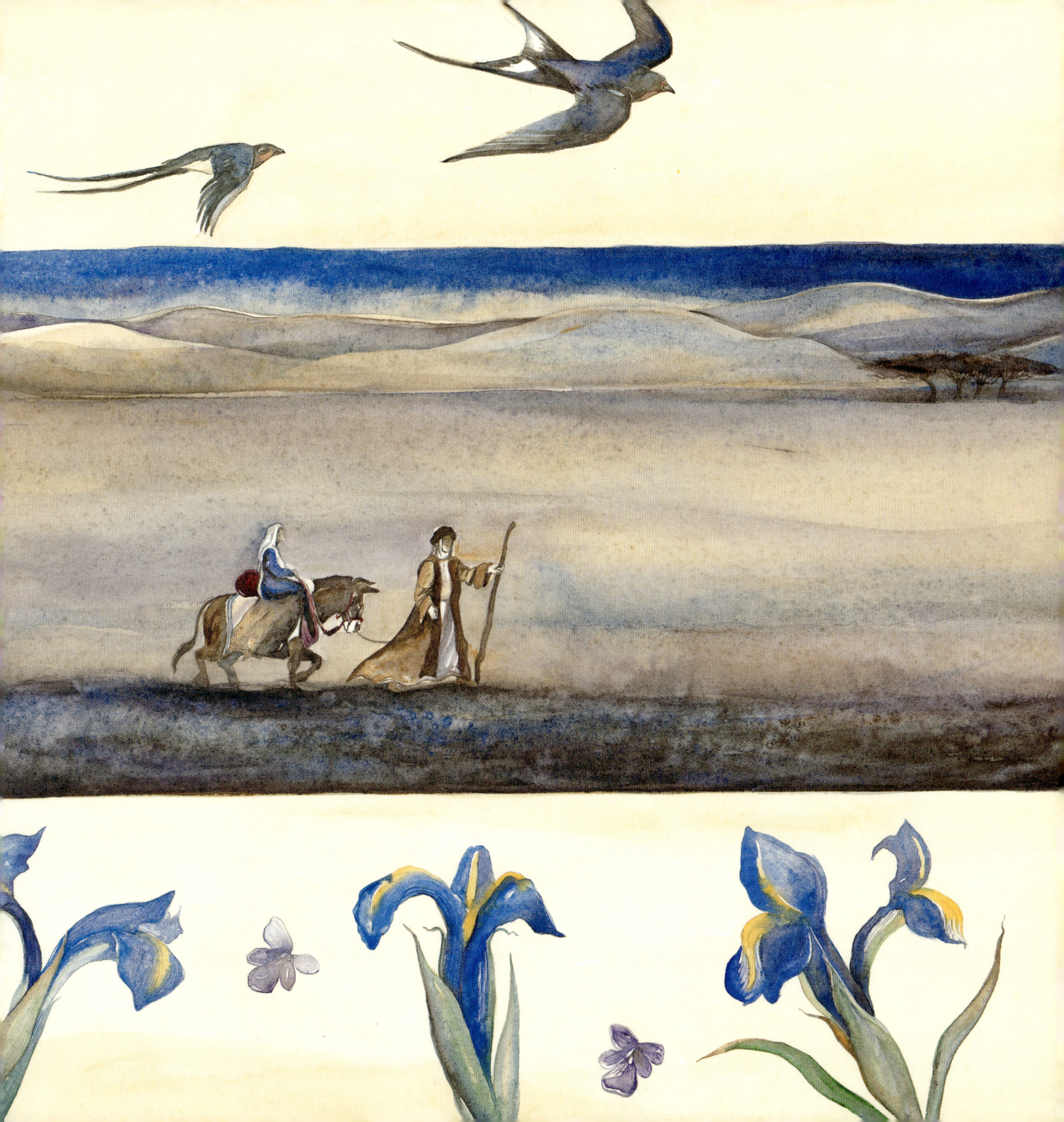

Little one,
 we knew you'd come.

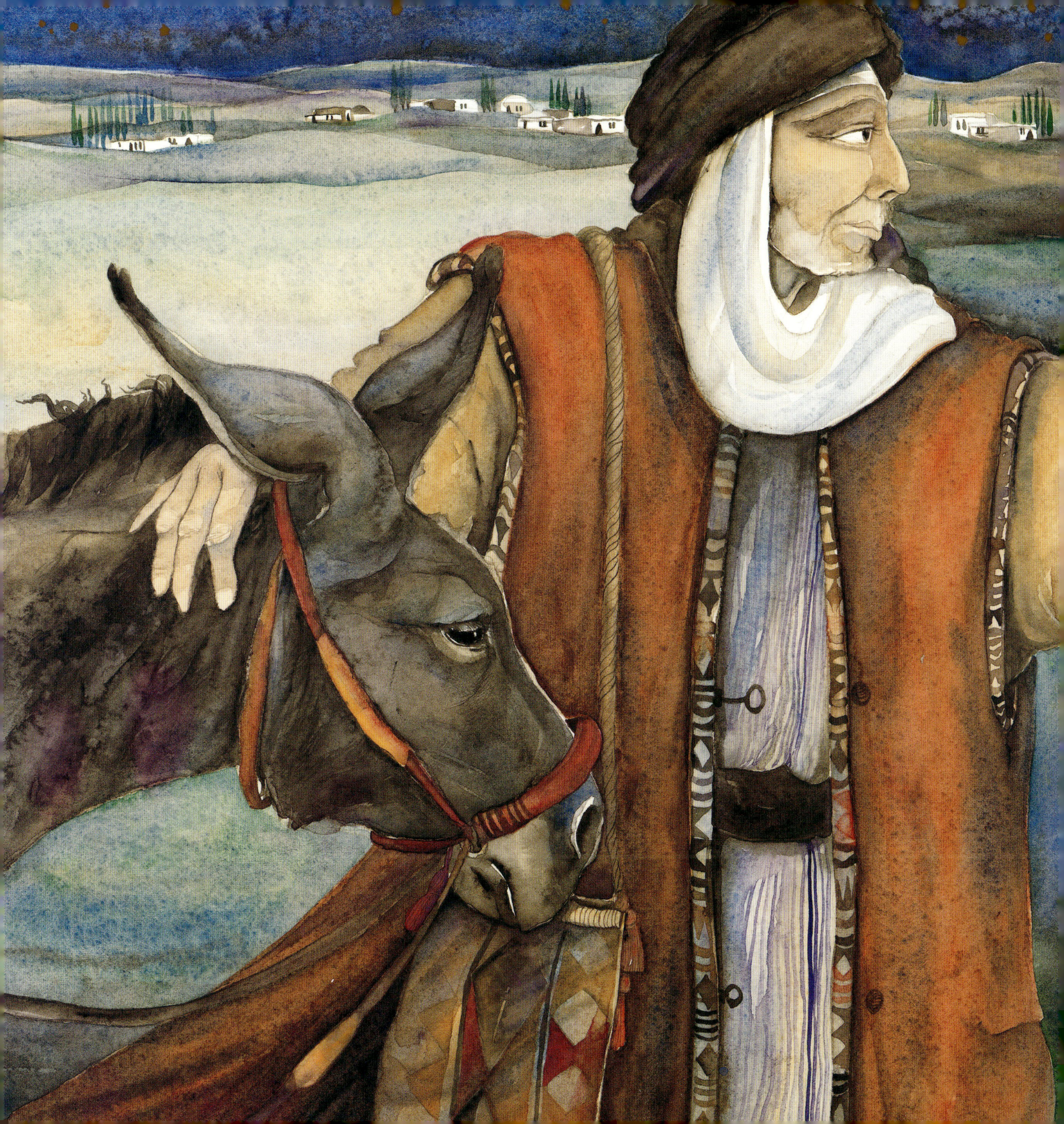

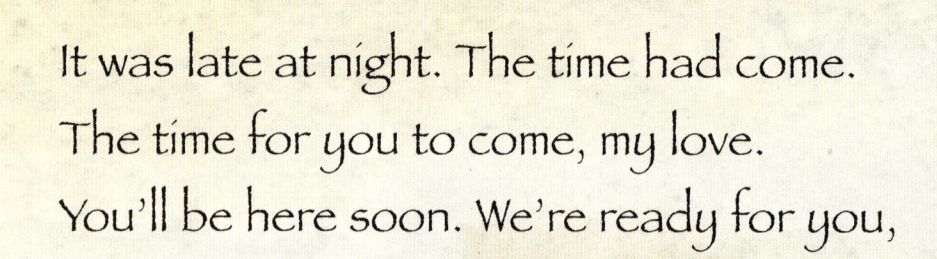

It was late at night. The time had come.
The time for you to come, my love.
You'll be here soon. We're ready for you,

And the day that you'll be born.

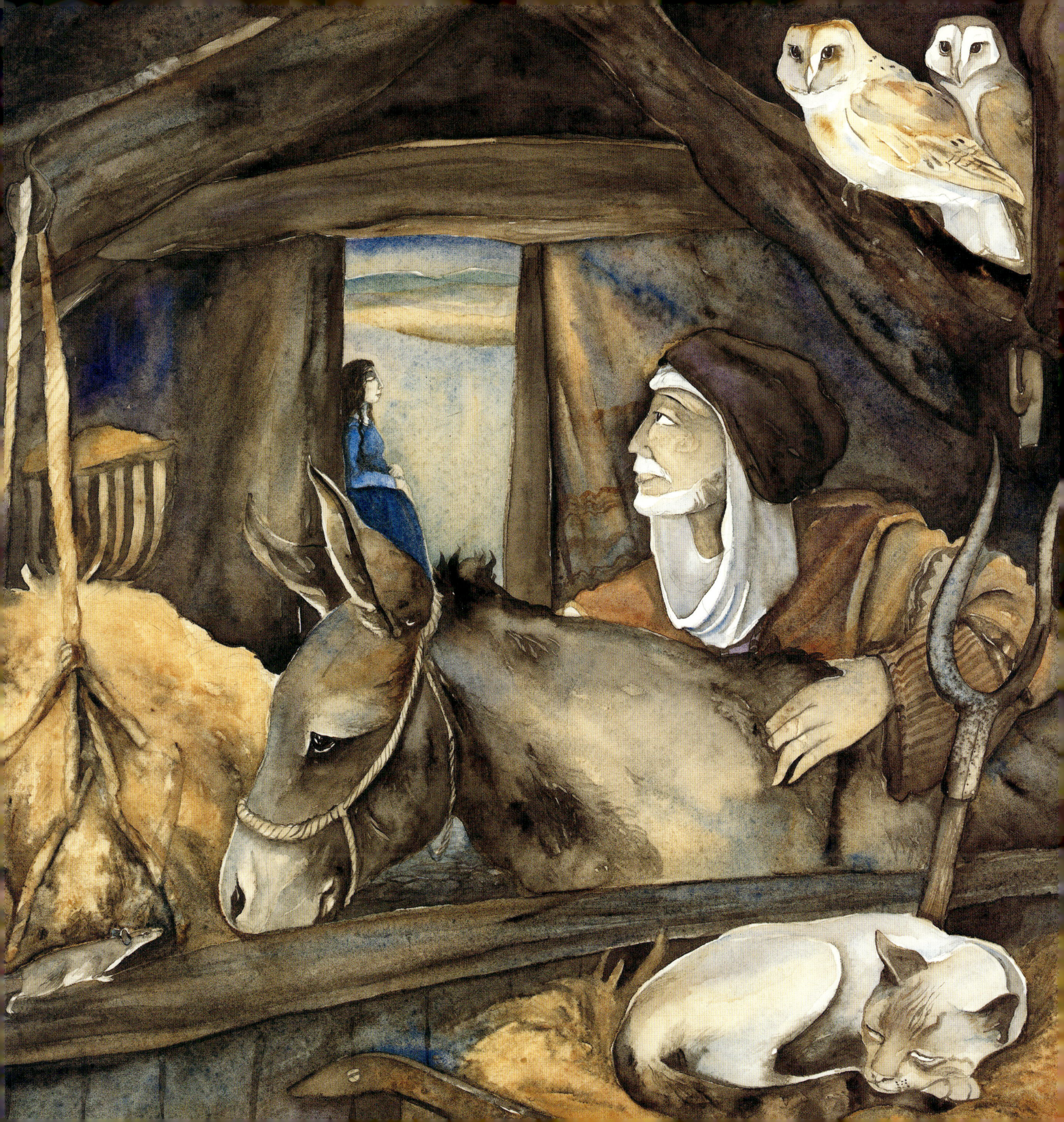

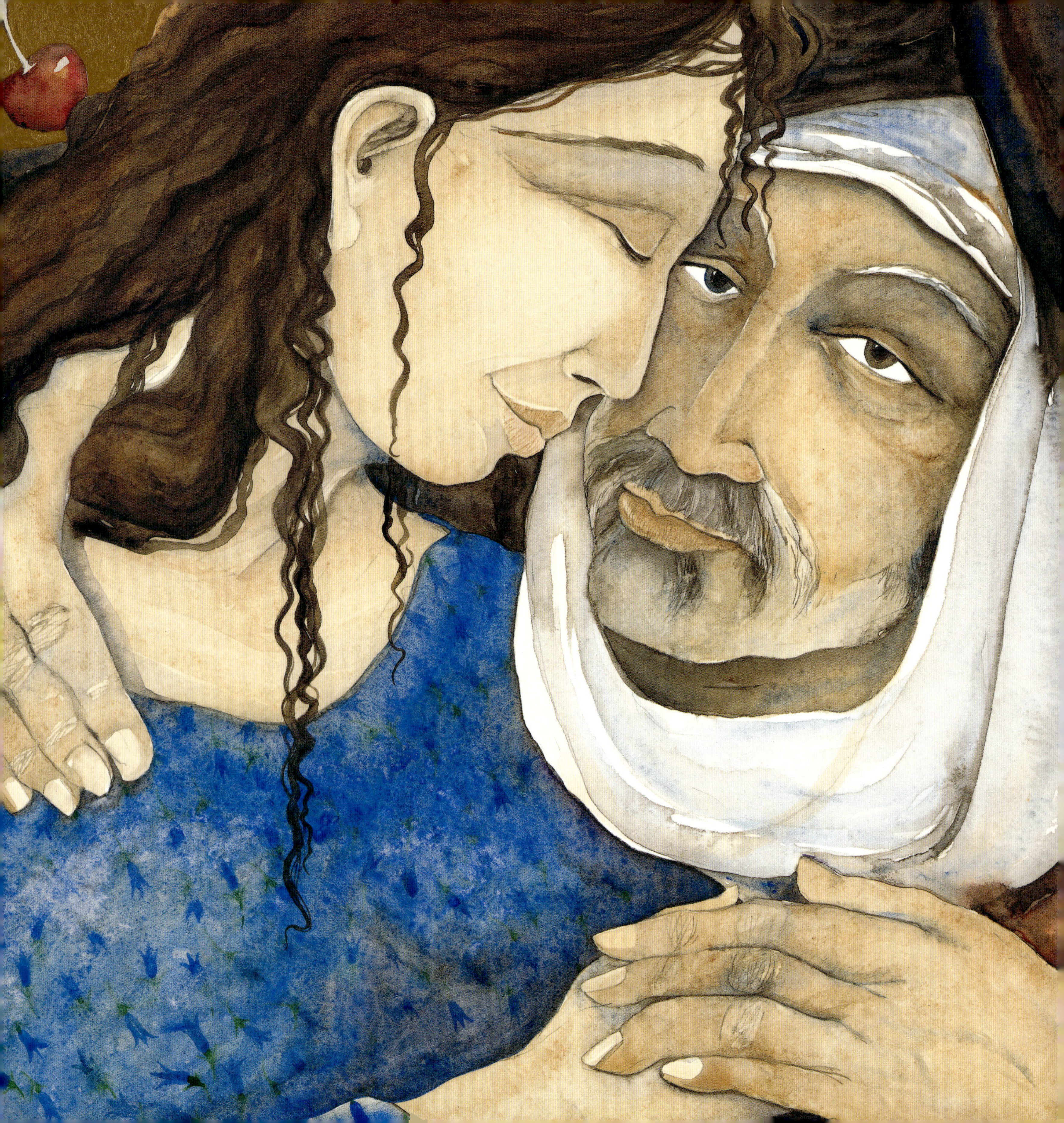

Little one,
　　　we knew you'd come.

By silver stars and golden moon,
At break of dawn, you came.
Kiss your nose, those tiny toes,

On the day that you were born.

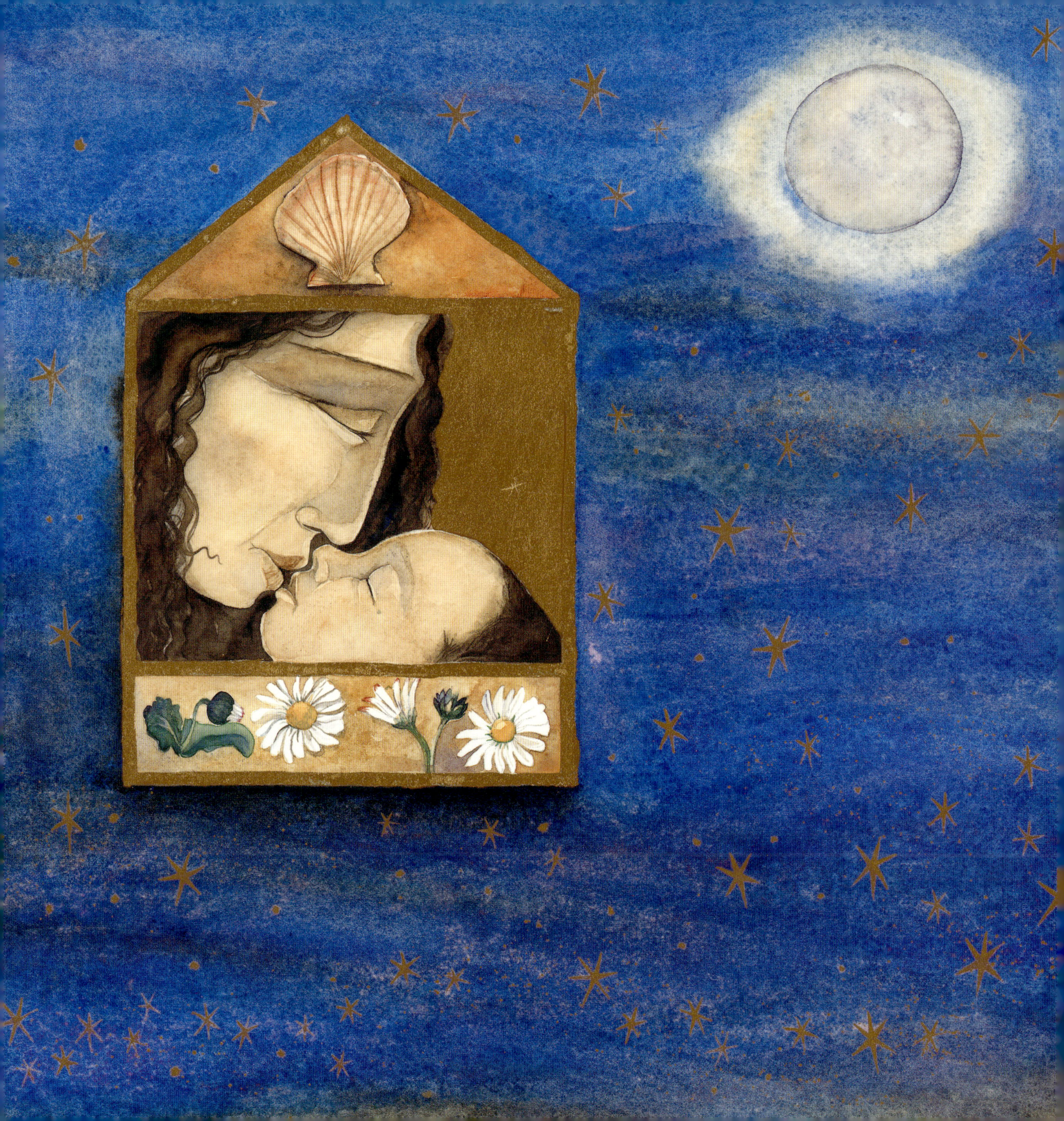

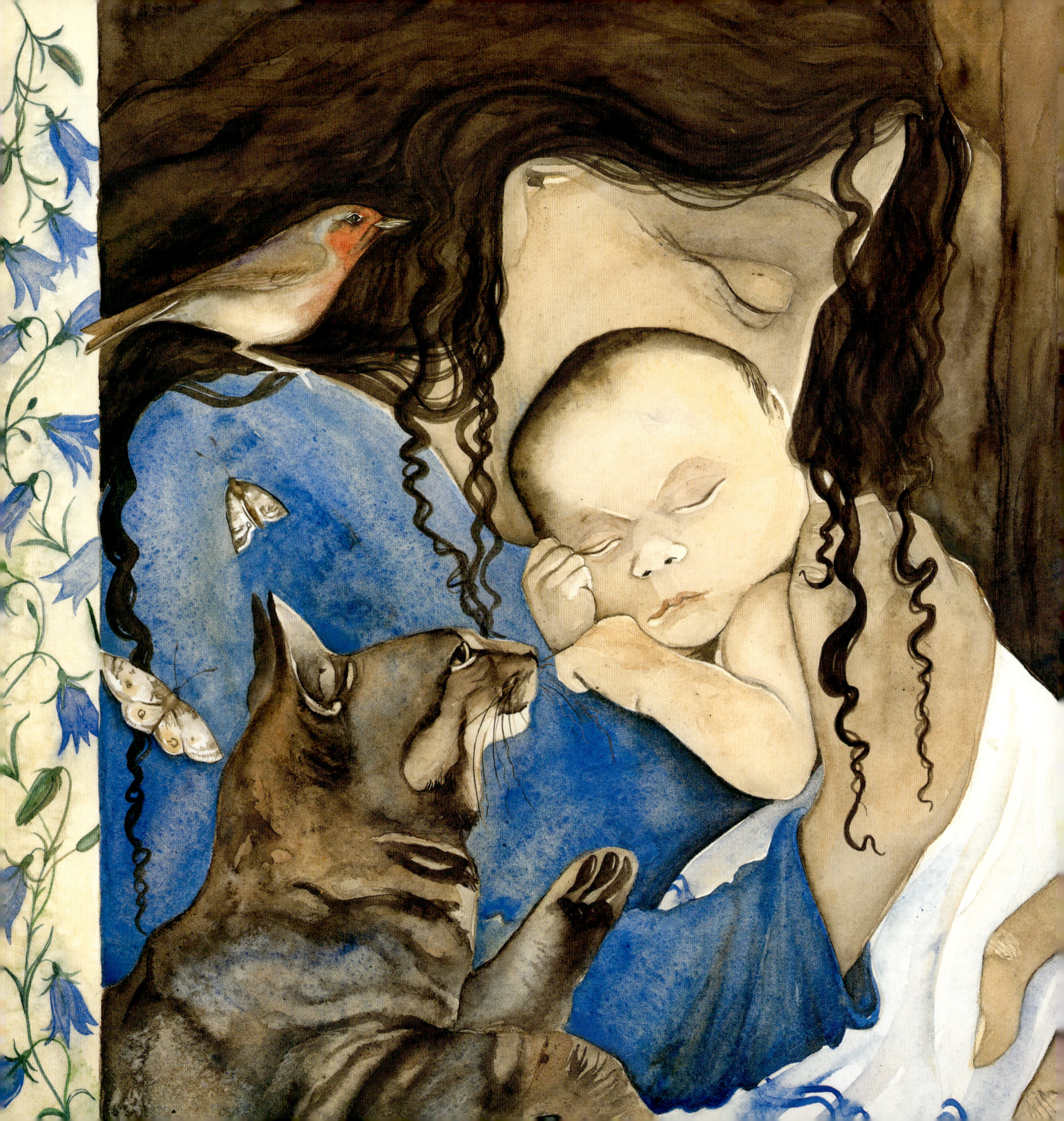

Little one,
     we knew you'd come.

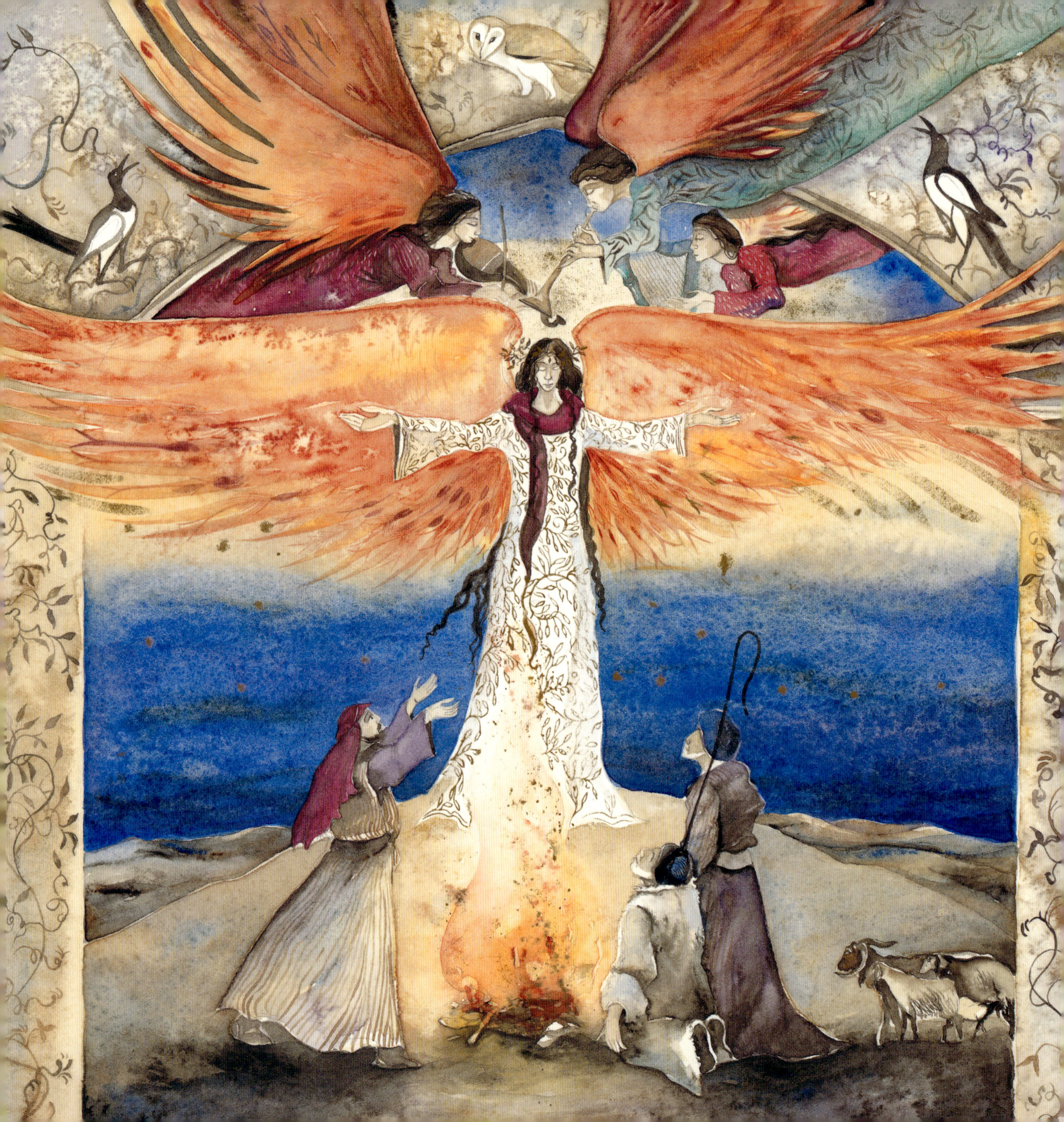

People were sleeping. We didn't care.
Good news, we sang, our baby is here!
Our baby has come, our darling one,

Oh, the day that you were born.

Little one,
    we knew you'd come.

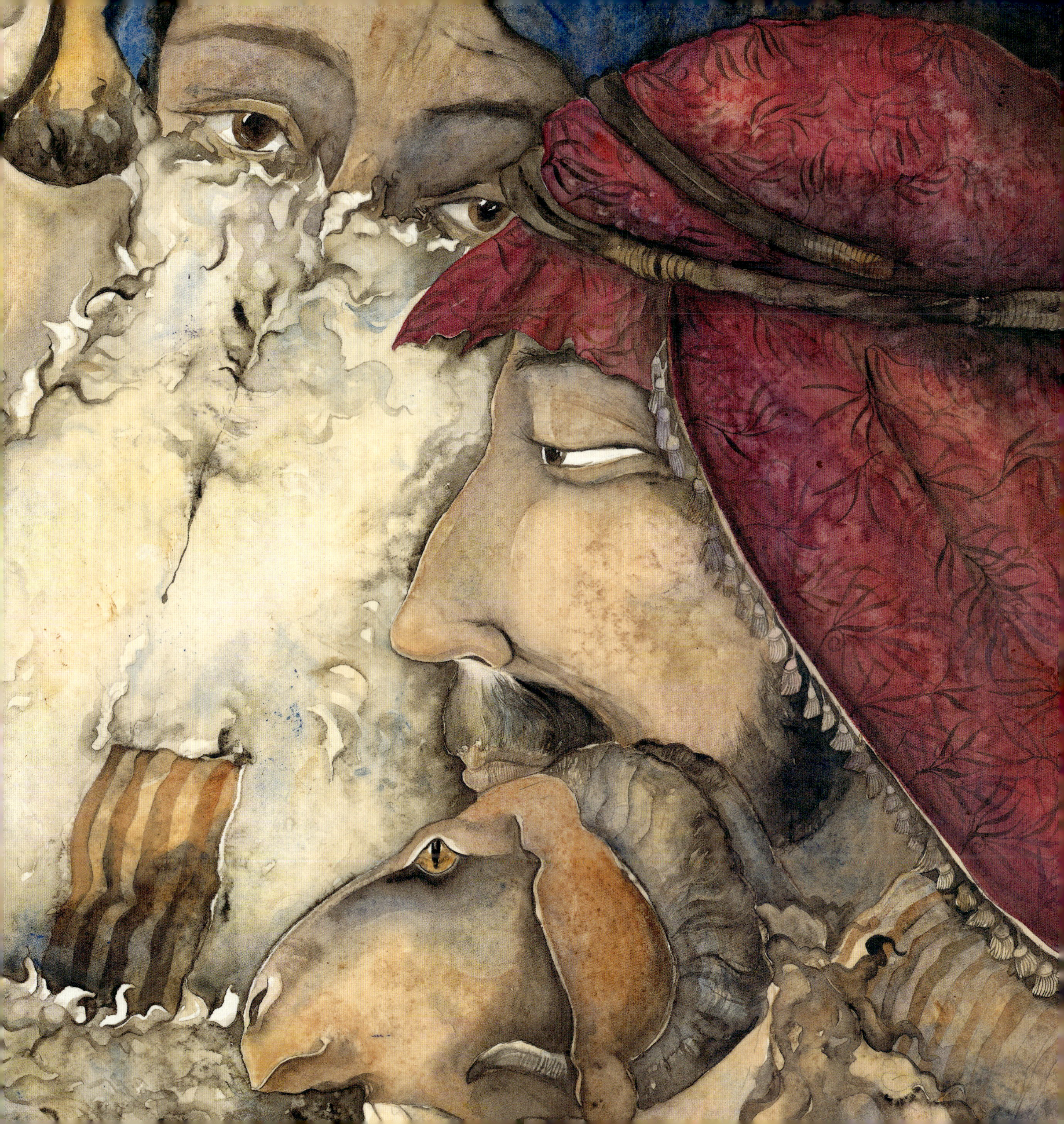

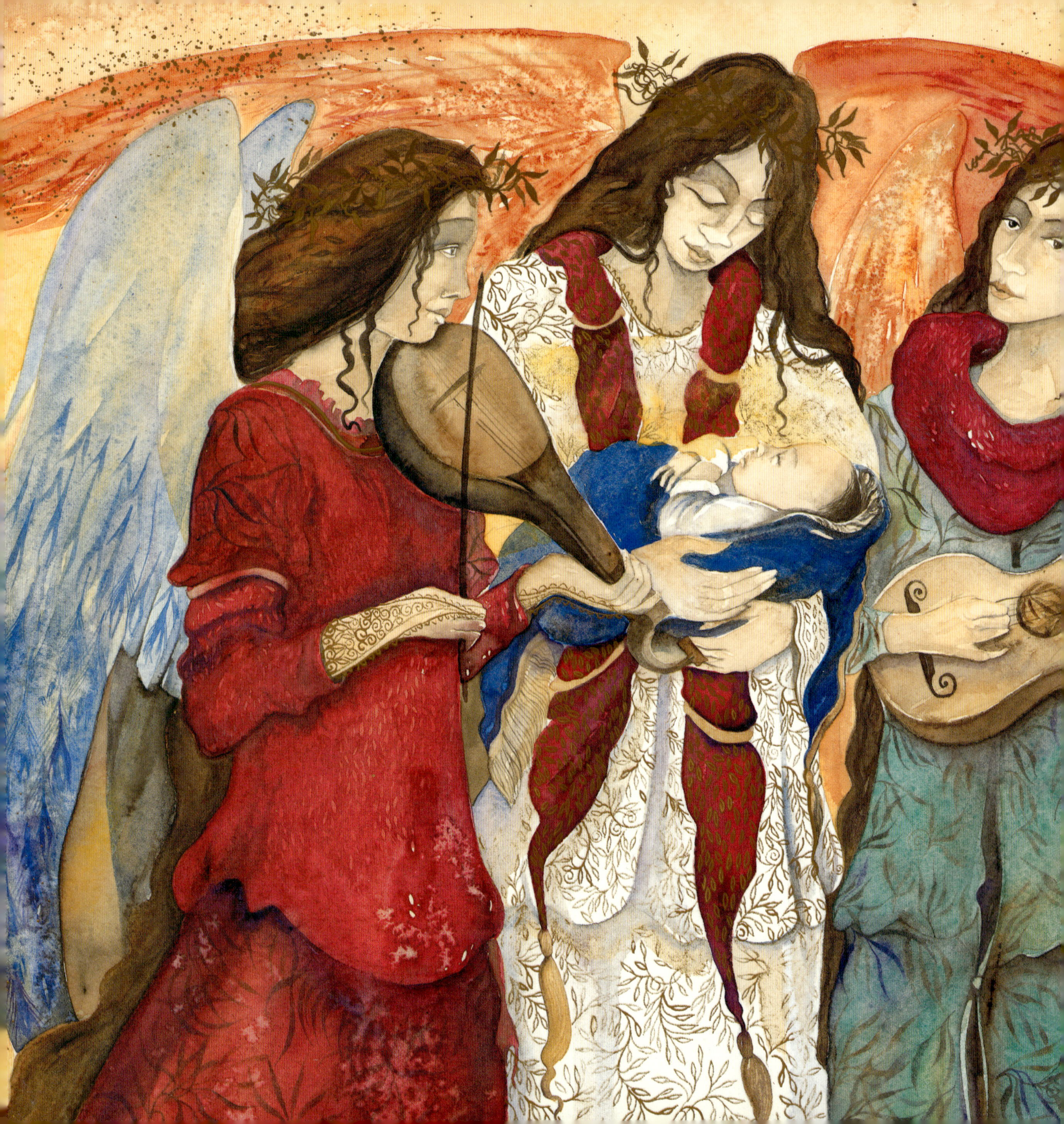

Kiss and cuddle and love the baby.
Scoop that baby up,
And softly sing a lullaby,

On the day that you were born.

Little one . . .

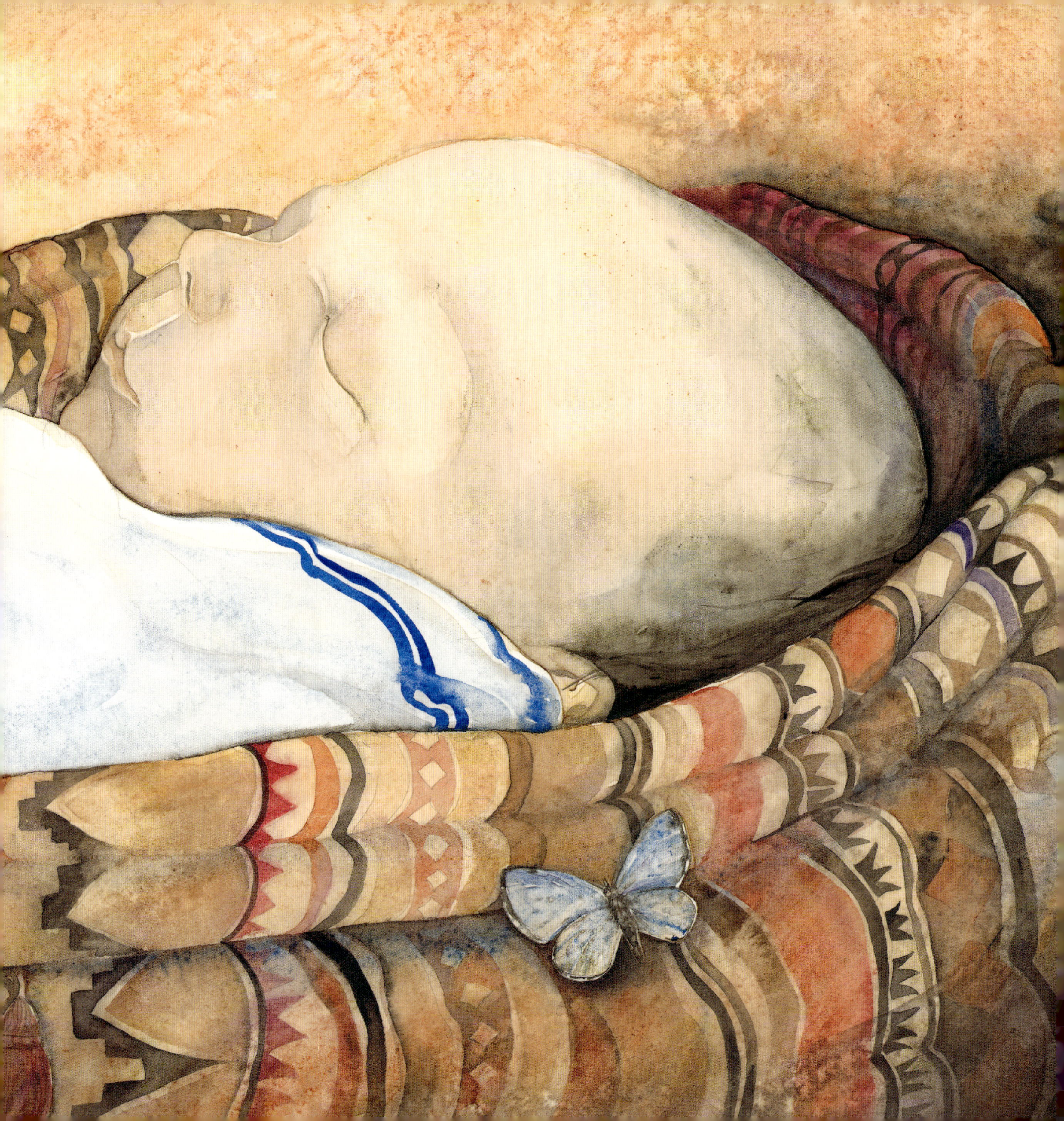

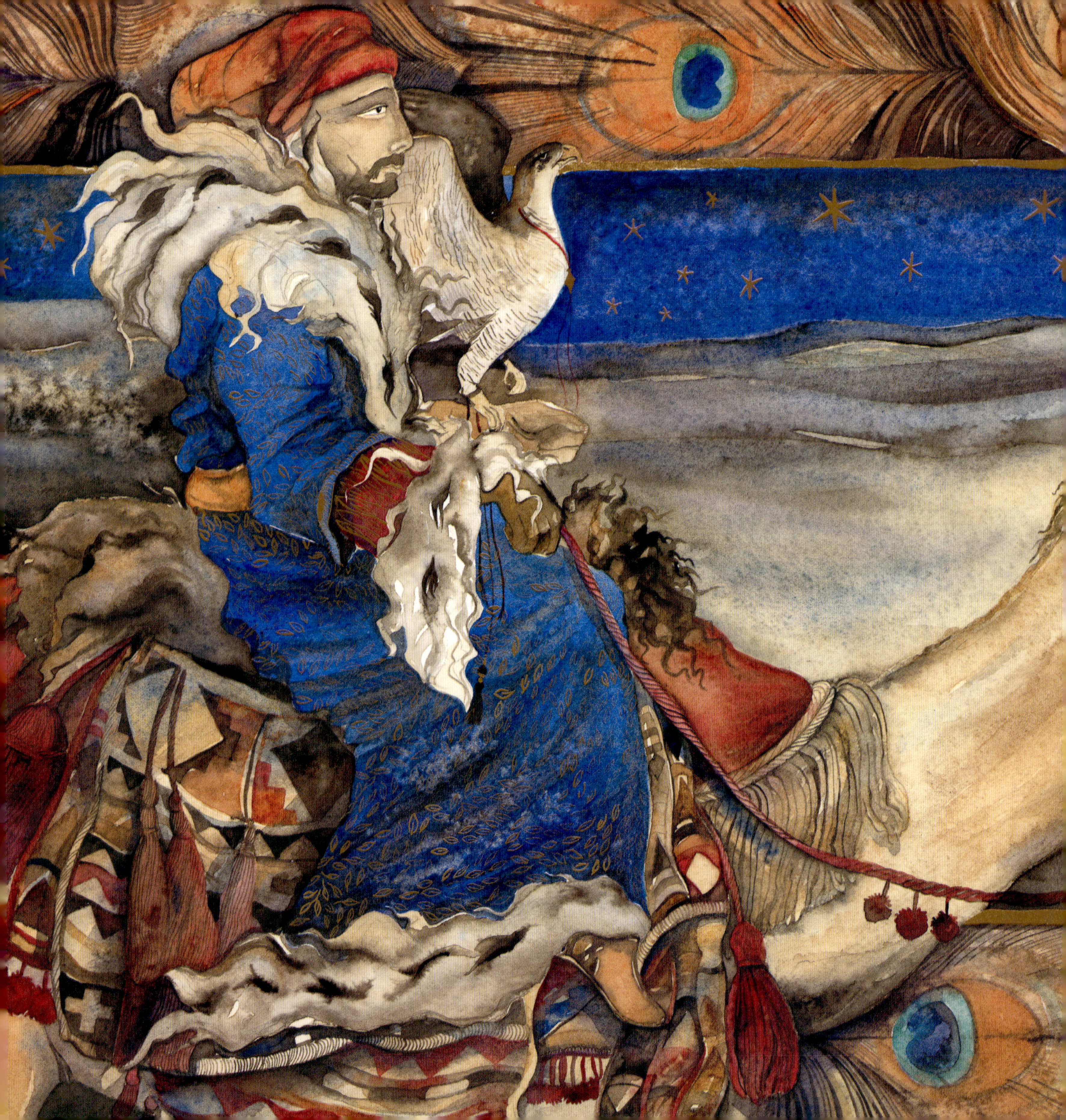

. . . we knew you'd come.

And every year, we remember you,
Our miracle child, our dreams come true.
Oh, how we thank Heaven for you,

And the day that you were born.

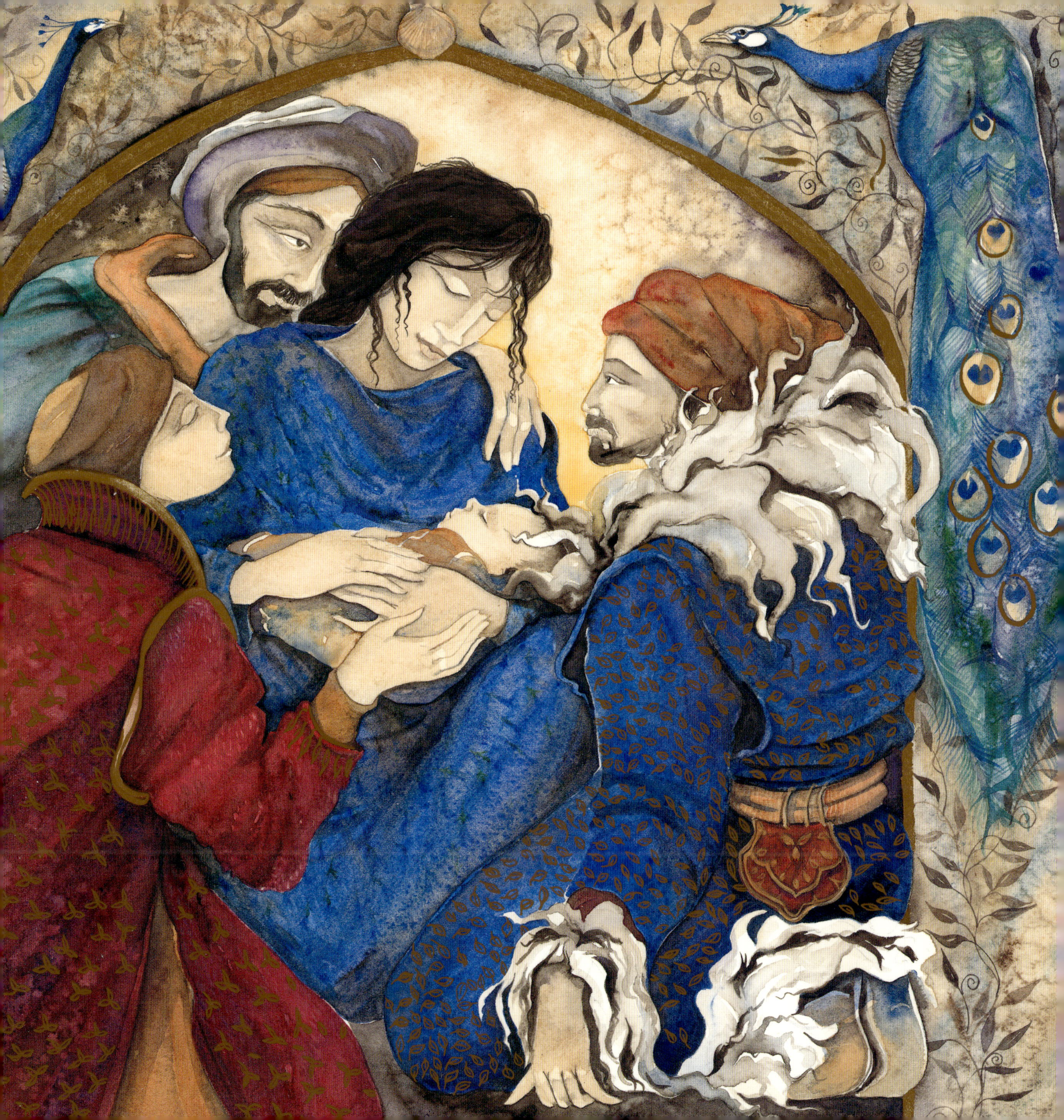

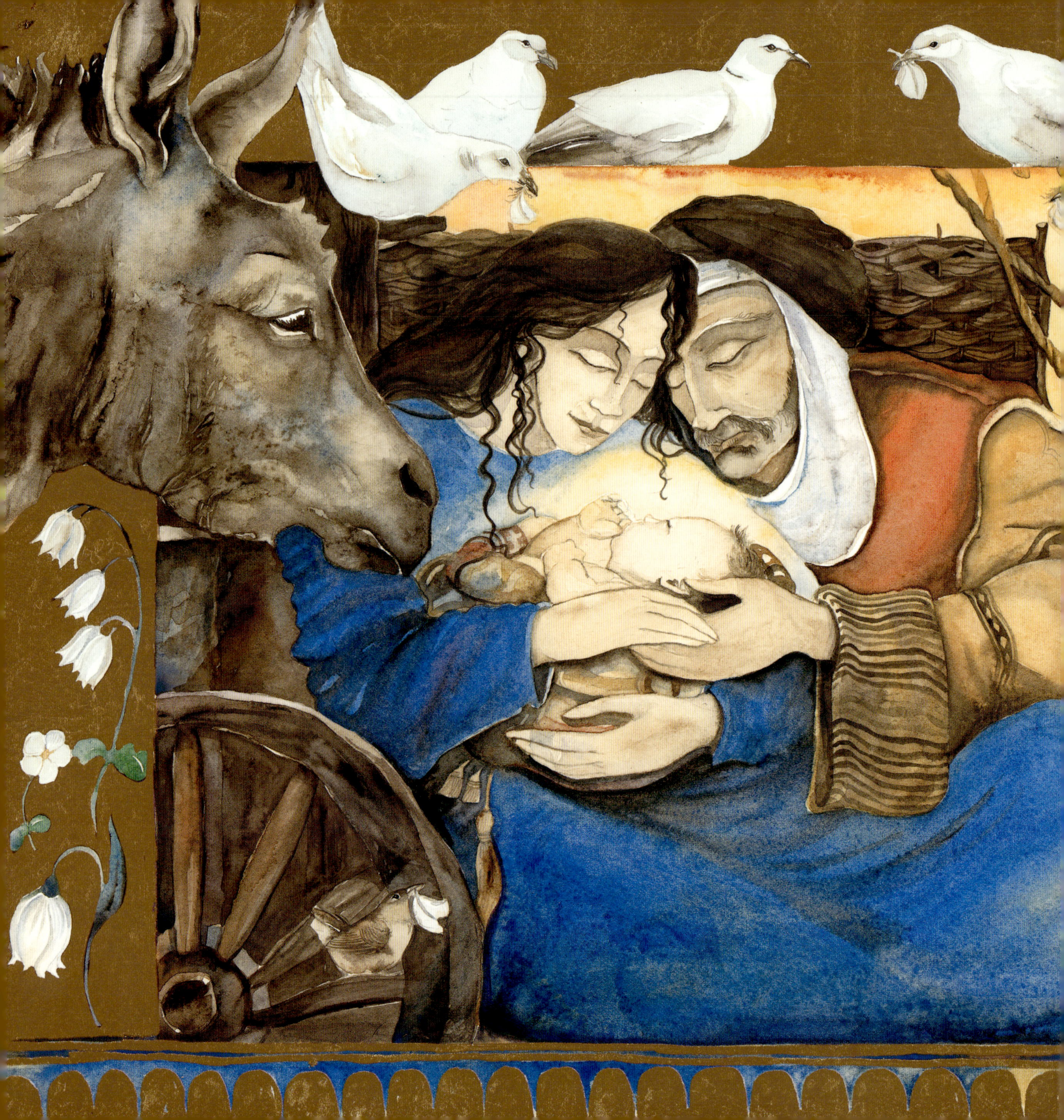

Little one,
 we're so glad you've come!

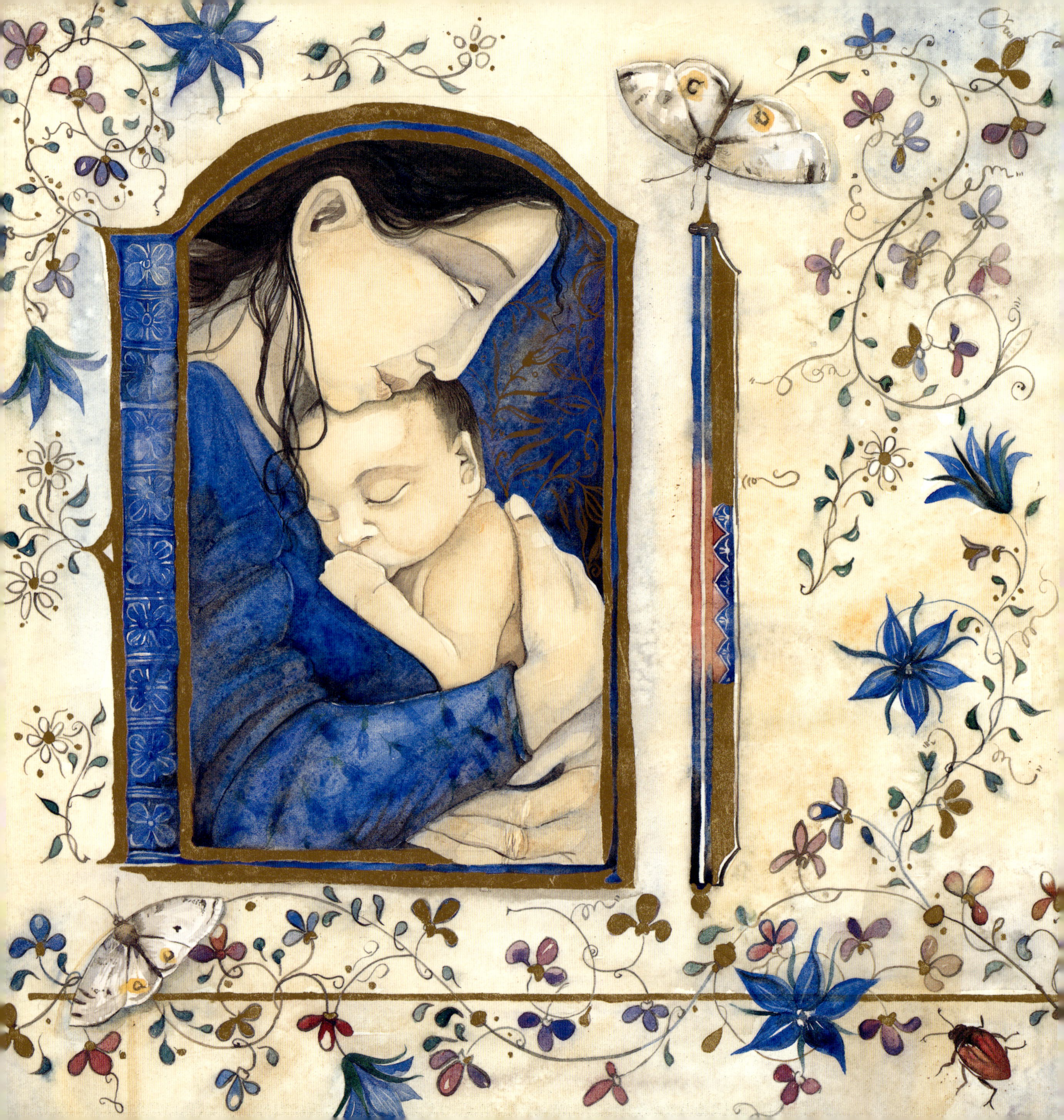